PRINCE PHILIP

WIT, WISDOM, BLUNDERS AND BLUSTERINGS

THE GREAT QUOTES

Dedication:

His Royal Highness The Prince Philip, Duke of Edinburgh, Earl of Merioneth, Baron Greenwich, Royal Knight of the Most Noble Order of the Garter, Extra Knight of the Most Ancient and Most Noble Order of the Thistle, Member of the Order of Merit, Grand Master and First and Principal Knight Grand Cross of the Most Excellent Order of the British Empire, Knight of the Order of Australia, Additional Member of the Order of New Zealand, Extra Companion of the Queen's Service Order, Royal Chief of the Order of Logohu, Extraordinary Companion of the Order of Canada, Extraordinary Commander of the Order of Military Merit, Lord of Her Majesty's Most Honourable Privy Council, Privy Councillor of the Queen's Privy Council for

Canada, Personal Aide-de-Camp to Her Majesty,
Lord High Admiral of the United Kingdom

INTRODUCTION

Prince Philip has has always stood out. In his younger years his dashing good looks, wild friends, glamorous lifestyle — not to mention his high-flying wife — drew the attention of not just the nation, but the world.

But it wasn't just his adventurous and glamorous lifestyle that drew curious eyes and an eager press ready to write about his every move. It was in fact often the lack of filter between his brilliant but excitable brain and mouth that drew the biggest gasps.

Collected here are the most memorable lines the Prince ever delivered, from wry witticisms to statements that were very much *of their time.*

MY MOST HONORED GUEST

"What are you doing here?"

Philip asked this of Simon Kelner, the republican editor of The Independent, at a Windsor Castle reception in 2002.

"I was invited, sir," replied the editor.

"Well, you didn't have to come."

CHINESE RELATIONS

"If you stay here much longer, you will go home with slitty eyes."

To 21-year-old Simon Kerby, a British student in China in 1986.

HOW TO TALK TO LADIES

"You are a woman, aren't you?"

He asked a Kenyan woman in 1984 during a visit.

HUNGRY IN HUNGARY

"You can't have been here that long, you haven't got a pot belly,"

To a British tourist in Budapest, in 1993.

ARGH ME HEARTIES!

"Aren't most of you descended from pirates?"

Residents of the Cayman Islands were asked in 1994.

DOGS FOR EATING

"Do you know they have eating dogs for the anorexic now?"

He quipped while talking to wheelchair-bound Susan Edwards with her guide dog Natalie in 2002.

ECONOMIC ADVICE FOR
STUDENTS

"Why don't you go and live in a hostel to save cash?"

Philip asked a poverty-stricken student in 1998.

DO YOU KNOW WHO I AM!?

"You bloody silly fool!"

Philip snapped at an elderly car park attendant who failed to recognize him in 1997 while visiting Cambridge University.

CHOP CHOP!

"Just take the fucking picture," he told the photographer in 2015 while visiting the RAF club.

THE BENEFITS AND DRAWBACKS
OF LEISURE

"A few years ago, everybody was saying we must have more leisure, everyone's working too much. Now that everybody's got more leisure time they are complaining they are unemployed."

Said during the recession in 1981.

HOLIDAYING IN THE USSR

"I would like to go to Russia very much –
although the bastards murdered half my
family."

He replied when asked in 1967 if he would
like to visit the USSR.

ON TAXES

"All money nowadays seems to be produced with a natural homing instinct for the Treasury."

Said in 1963 when asked about taxes.

THE IMPOVERISHED PRINCE

"We go into the red next year... I shall probably have to give up polo."

The Prince remarked on US television in
1969, moaning about the Royal Family's
finances.

THE DELIGHTS OF CANADA

"We don't come here for our health. We can think of other ways of enjoying ourselves."

The Prince said, somewhat tactlessly, about a trip to Canada in 1976.

NURSING HOME SPEEDBUMP

"Do people trip over you?"

The Prince joked to a wheelchair using resident of a nursing home in 2002.

MINK KNICKERS

"You're not wearing mink knickers, are you?"

Philip asked Serena French, a fashion writer, at a WWF event in 1993.

DEMOLITION DERBY SCOOTER

"How many people have you knocked over this morning on that thing?"

He asked mobility scooter user David Miller in 2012.

THE CULINARY TALENTS OF THE BRITISH FEMALE

"British women can't cook."

This wisdom was imparted to the Scottish Women's Institute in 1961.

MILLINER MUSINGS

"Where did you get that hat?"

Philip asked during his wife's Coronation.

THE CRUMBLING CLASS SYSTEM

"People think there's a rigid class system here, but dukes have even been known to marry chorus girls. Some have even married Americans."

Said in 2000.

CARIBBEAN HOSPITAL WORKERS DON'T KNOW HOW GOOD THEY HAVE IT

"You have mosquitoes. I have the Press."

Philip said to the matron of a hospital in the Caribbean in 1966.

CANNIBALS IN THE PACIFIC

"You managed not to get eaten then?"

To a British backpacker who trekked across Papua New Guinea in 1998.

AND WOULD YOU DANCE FOR ME?

"Is it a strip club?"

Philip asked a female Sea Cadet who had said to him that she worked in a nightclub.

MY WIFE IS NOT A PROSTITUTE, BUT…

"I don't think a prostitute is more moral than a wife, but they are doing the same thing."

This remark was made while discussing blood sports in 1988.

FAMILY FORTUNES

"Are you all one family?"

Philip asked the members of a multi-ethnic dance troupe at the 2009 Royal Variety Performance.

MS FEMINISM 2000

"Ah, so this is feminist corner then."

Prince Philip asked a group of female MPs who used the title "Ms" on their name badges at a Palace event in 2000.

BEDDING PROBLEMS

"Every time I talk to a woman they say I've been to bed with her. Well I'm bloody flattered at my age to think some girl is interested in me."

-2006

DO POLITICIANS WEAR TARTAN UNDERWEAR?

"Do you have any knickers in that material?"

The Prince asked this of Scottish Tory leader Annabel Goldie, while the pair of them admired tartan made for the Pope.

WHAT'S THE DIFFERENCE BETWEEN A PROSTITUTE AND A SOLICITOR?

"I thought it was against the law these days for a woman to solicit."

This was said to a woman solicitor.

EXPERT ADVICE

"I have never been noticeably reticent about talking on subjects about which I know nothing."

Philip said to a group of industrialists in 1961.

MY CHARMING DAUGHTER

"If it doesn't fart or eat hay, she isn't interested."

Philip was talking about his daughter, Princess Anne, who competed in equestrian events at the 1976 Olympics.

DON'T TALK BACK!

"Yak, yak, yak; come on get a move on."

Prince Philip said to the Queen on board the royal yacht *Britannia* while her majesty was talking to their hosts in Belize in 1994.

DRUMMING SOME SENSE
INTO THEM

"Deaf? If you're near there, no wonder you are deaf."

He said in 2000 to a group of deaf children standing near a Caribbean steel drum group.

PROMOTING LITERACY

"Ah you're the one who wrote the letter. So you can write then? Ha, ha! Well done."

He said to a 14 year old boy from Romsford.

DRUGS AND YOUTH CULTURE

"So who's on drugs here?... HE looks as if he's on drugs."

The Prince indicated a fourteen year old member of a Bangladeshi youth club in 2002.

ADVICE ON ASTRONAUT TRAINING

"You could do with losing a little bit of weight."

The prince remarked to a thirteen year old hopeful future astronaut.

THE JOYS OF CHILDREN

"Holidays are curious things, aren't they? You send children to school to get them out of your hair. Then they come back and make life difficult for parents. That is why holidays are set so they are just about the limit of your endurance."

Philip said to a group of schoolchildren in 2000.

ZIPPEDY-DOO-DA

"I would be arrested if I unzipped that dress."

Philip said to a supporter in Bromley during a Diamond Jubilee event.

SCOTTISH RELATIONS

"How do you keep the natives off the booze long enough to pass the test?"

He asked a Scottish driving instructor in 1995.

CONCERN FOR FEMALE
FINANCIAL SECURITY

"Who do you sponge off?"

Philip asked women at a Barking and Dagenham community centre in 2015.

/~ IN THE NAVY… ~/

"I'd much rather have stayed in the Navy, frankly."

Philip said in 1992 on his role as consort.

AUSTRALIAN MUSICAL TALENT IS SUSPECT

"You were playing your instruments? Or do you have tape recorders under your seats?"

He asked an Australian school orchestra in 2002.

ABORIGINAL TRADITIONS

"Do you still throw spears at each other?"

William Brin, an Aboriginal leader was asked in 2002 at the Aboriginal Cultural Park in Queensland.

THE JEWEL OF THE MIDLANDS

"And what exotic part of the world do you come from?"

Philip asked Tory politician Lord Taylor of Warwick in 1999.

"Birmingham," the politician replied.

THE DELIGHTS OF EDUCATION IN SCOTLAND

"Only a Scotsman can really survive a Scottish education."

Philip quipped in 1953 when he was made Chancellor of Edinburgh University.

A BACKHANDED COMPLIMENT

"Well, that's more than you know about anything else then."

Philip said in 2004 to Michael Burke, after the BBC newsreader said he did in fact know about the Duke of Edinburgh's Gold Awards

THE WONDERS OF A GLOBAL
LABOUR MARKET

"The Philippines must be half empty, you're all here running the NHS."

Philip said to a Filipino nurse at Luton and Dunstable University Hospital in 2016.

FOOL!

"Damn fool question!"

Philip said contemptuously to BBC journalist Caroline Wyatt who had attempted to ask the Queen how she was enjoying Paris during a 2006 visit.

THEY WANTED TO FIT ONE TO MY CAR…

"A pissometer?"

Philip joked when being shown a piezometer water gauge in 2000.

JUDGING BOOKS BY THEIR COVERS

"Where are you from?" he asked the editor of the Sun newspaper.

On being informed of the gentleman's occupation, he replied, "Oh, no...one can't tell from the outside."

WHAT, THESE SILLY OLD THINGS?

"My son...er...owns them."

Philip said when asked whether he knew of the Scilly Isles.

MY SON'S BOUDOIR

"It looks like a tart's bedroom."

Philip described thusly the plans for the Duke and Duchess of York's house at Sunninghill Park.

AQUATIC FARMING CRITIQUE

"Oh! You are the people ruining the rivers and the environment."

Philip remarked to three young workers at a Scottish fish farm in 1999 near Holyrood Palace.

CATTLE CLASS

"If you travel as much as we do you appreciate the improvements in aircraft design of less noise and more comfort. Provided you don't travel in something called Economy Class, which sounds ghastly."

Aircraft Research Association, 2002.

MARRIAGE ADVICE

"Tolerance is the one essential ingredient ... You can take it from me that the Queen has the quality of tolerance in abundance."

This advice on a successful marriage was given in 1997.

THE YOUTH OF TODAY

"Young people are the same as they always were. They are just as ignorant."

The Prince made this remark while cele-brating the 50th anniversary of the young people's Duke of Edinburgh Awards scheme.

I'LL GET MY MAN TO GIVE YOU A STICKER

"It looks like the kind of thing my daughter would bring back from her school art lessons."

Philip remarked on viewing some "primitive" Ethiopian art in 1965.

AGING

"Bits are beginning to drop off."

In 2011, just before turning ninety.

EMBARRASSING? ME? NOT ANYMORE!

"I reckon I have done something right if I don't appear in the media. So I've retreated – quite consciously – so as not to be an embarrassment."

Philip said in 2006.

WITH THIS METHOD, YOU CAN GET AWAY WITH SAYING ANYTHING

"It's my custom to say something flattering to begin with so I shall be excused if I put my foot in it later on."

Philip said in 1956.

WISDOM FOR DENTISTS

"Dentopedology is the science of opening your mouth and putting your foot in it, a science which I have practiced for a good many years."

To the General Dental Council in 1960.

I HAVE THE BEST STAFF

"You're just a silly little Whitehall twit: you don't trust me and I don't trust you."

Philip said to Sir Rennie Maudslay, Keeper of the Privy Purse, in the mid 1970s.

THE PROBLEM WITH LONDON

"The problem with London is the tourists. They cause the congestion. If we could just stop the tourism, we could stop the congestion."

Philip remarked at the opening of London's new City Hall in 2002.

SEEKING ADVICE FROM TOM JONES

"What do you gargle with – pebbles?"

Philip asked Tom Jones after the Royal Variety Performance in 1969. He went on to add:

"It is very difficult at all to see how it is possible to become immensely valuable by singing what I think are the most hideous songs."

YOUR NAME IS AWFULLY COMMON

"There's a lot of your family in tonight."

Philip said to Atul Patel during a 2009 Buckingham Palace event for 400 influential British Indians.

NEXT DOOR NEIGHBOR
FROM HELL

"Oh, it's you that owns that ghastly car is it? We often see it when driving to Windsor Castle."

Philip said to his neighbor, the singer Elton John, after hearing he had sold the Watford FC-themed Aston Martin in 2001.

CROCODILE HUNTER

"It's not a very big one, but at least it's dead and it took an awful lot of killing!"

Philip boasted of his hunting prowess in The Gambia in 1957.

ON YOUTH MUSIC, LIKE
ELTON JOHN

"I wish he'd turn the microphone off!"

Philip said of Elton John's time on the stage at
the 2001 73rd Royal Variety Show.

THE DELIGHTS OF CHINESE CUISINE

"If it has four legs and it is not a chair, if it has got two wings and it flies but is not an aeroplane and if it swims and it is not a submarine, the Cantonese will eat it."

OR WOULD YOU PREFER I CALL YOU FUHRER?

"Reichskanzler," was the title Philip used to address German chancellor Helmut Kohl in 1997. The title was last used by Hitler.

SARTORIAL OBSERVATION

"You look like you're ready for bed!"

Philip quipped to the traditional robe-wearing President of Nigeria in 2003.

MADONNA'S HOLY RACKET

"Are we going to need ear plugs?"

Philip inquired after being told that Madonna was to perform the new James Bond theme song in 2002.

THIS IS YOUR LINE OF WORK

"Can you fix my DVD player?"

Philip asked this of actress Cate Blanchett because she worked "in the film industry" in 2008. Upon seeing her evident confusion, he went on to ask:

"There's a cord sticking out of the back. Might you tell me where it goes?"

GUN CONTROL? WHAT ABOUT CRICKET BAT CONTROL?

"If a cricketer, for instance, suddenly decided to go into a school and batter a lot of people to death with a cricket bat, which he could do very easily, I mean, are you going to ban cricket bats?"

Philip mused on potential new gun control measures after the Dunblane Massacre of 1996.

YOU THINK YOU'VE HAD IT HARD? WAIT UNTIL YOU HEAR WHAT HAPPENED TO MY CASTLE!

"People usually say that after a fire it is water damage that is the worst. We are still drying out Windsor Castle."

Philip rather tactlessly made this remark to survivors of the Lockerbie bombings in 1993.

THE SOLEMNITY OF WREATH LAYING

"Any bloody fool can lay a wreath at the thingamy."

Philip told interviewer Jeremy Paxman in 2006.

STRESS RELIEF

"We didn't have counsellors rushing around every time somebody let off a gun. You just got on with it!"

Philip made this remark while discussing stress counseling for members of the armed forces in 1995.

ARE ALL GINGERS TERRORISTS?

"Is that a terrorist?"

Philip asked this on New Year's Eve in 2017 when he spotted a tall man with a long red beard near the church at Sandringham.

BREEDING UNLIKE RABBITS

"Don't feed your rabbits pawpaw fruit – it acts as a contraceptive. Then again, it might not work on rabbits."

These wise words were shared with a Caribbean rabbit breeder in Anguilla in 1994.

I DON'T NEED ANY NEW STIS, THANK YOU VERY MUCH

"Oh no, I might catch some ghastly disease."

Prince Philip said this while turning down the chance to stroke a koala bear during a 1992 visit to Australia.

SAVE THE BIRDS!

"Cats kill far more birds than men. Why don't you have a slogan: 'Kill a cat and save a bird?'"

To wildlife campaigners in 1965.

I'M STARVING!

"Bugger the table plan, give me my dinner!"

Philip said at a dinner party in 2004.

IS THIS YOUR WIND FARM?

"[Wind farms] are absolutely useless and an absolute disgrace."

Philip informed the managing director of a wind farm in 2011.

YOU COOKED IT, DID YOU?

"No, I would probably end up spitting it out over everybody."

Philip responds to some fresh cooked seafood prepared by the award winning chef, Rick Stein in 2000.

**AND TO MY GRACIOUS HOSTS, I
WOULD LIKE TO SAY…**

"Your country is one of the most notorious
centres of trading in endangered species."

Philip said this to his hosts in Thailand
where he was accepting a conservation
award.

THE JOYS OF DICTATORSHIPS

"It's a pleasure to be in a country that isn't ruled by its people."

Philip remarked to the Paraguay dictator General Stroessner.

YOU WANT FASHION DESIGN ADVICE?

"Well, you didn't design your beard too well, did you? You really must try better with your beard."

Philip gave this advice to a young fashion designer being received at Buckingham Palace in 2009.

ROBOT (RE)PRODUCTION

"They're not mating are they?"

Philip asked when he observed two robots bumping into each other during a 2000 visit to the Science Museum in London.

INTERNATIONAL DIPLOMACY

"Can you tell the difference between them?"

Philip asked President Obama in 2009 who had just told the prince that he had breakfast with the leaders of the UK, China and Russia.

FIRE SAFETY

"[Smoke alarms are] a damn nuisance – I've got one in my bathroom and every time I run my bath the steam sets it off."

This unfortunate remarked was made to a woman who lost two sons to a fire in 1998.

THE NEW EMBASSY

"It's a vast waste of space."

Philip judged the new £18 million British Embassy in Berlin in 2000 during a visit with the Queen to formally open the building.

I HAD A VISIT FROM THE AMBASSADOR AND ALL I GOT WAS THIS STUPID HAMPER

"Where's the Southern Comfort?"

Philip asked of his American guest when gifted with a hamper by the American ambassador in 1999.

FRENCH SO-CALLED CUISINE

"The French don't know how to cook breakfast."

Philip remarked in 2002, after consuming a light petit dejeneur of bacon, eggs, smoked salmon, kedgeree, croissants and pain au chocolate.

THE FOOD IN MY PALACE

"I never see any home cooking – all I get is fancy stuff."

Philip made this complaint in 1962 while talking about the cuisine at Buckingham Palace.

COWBOYS AND INDIANS

"It looks as though it was put in by an Indian."

The Prince said about a fuse box at a Scottish factory in 1999. The Prince, realizing that he had perhaps misspoken, later went on to clarify:

"I meant to say cowboys. I just got my cowboys and Indians mixed up."

Printed in Great Britain
by Amazon